THE EASY W
TO LEARN HOW TO PLAY
THE UKULELE!

by
Christopher Richard

ABOUT THE AUTHOR

Christopher Richard is a musician/producer/songwriter who has over thirty years experience playing the guitar and performing with several Pittsburgh area rock groups and teaching guitar lessons at his studio in New Brighton, PA.

TABLE OF CONTENTS

ALPHABETICAL LIST OF SONGS
(Chords Used)

INTRODUCTION

The Ukulele has enjoyed a resurgence in popularity thanks to a number of things. Not only does its smaller, lighter body and soft nylon strings make it much easier to handle than a standard guitar, but most of the main music chords are a lot easier to learn and play, often using only one or two fingers instead of three or four. It is also a very popular instrument with many contemporary music artists and relatively inexpensive to purchase.

This guide will show you everything you need to get started on the ukulele. It is aimed at beginners of all ages with easy step by step instructions, pictures and illustrations to help you play right away, plus, it includes twenty three classic songs to play and enjoy!

So, go ahead and get started. You'll be playing in no time.

CHOOSING A UKULELE

It is usually a good idea to start out with an acoustic ukulele, if for no other reason than you will not need to buy an additional amplifier or cable to play it. Besides, the method of playing with strings and frets is basically the same for both acoustic and electric and you can always invest in an electric ukulele later if you decide to stick with it.

The price of ukuleles ranges from under $25 for beginner models to up in the hundreds for professional models depending on several factors, including the quality of the wood, the workmanship involved and the brand name. The most popular choice of ukulele is the acoustic soprano style. Here are a few good choices for an affordable beginner ukulele that are available from Amazon.com:

Mugig
Glossy Ukulele
Amazon Price: $39.99
ASIN: B0722WW8SR

Kala
Mahogany Ukulele
Amazon Price: $59.99
ASIN: B01F543PAW

Donner
Concert Ukulele
Amazon Price: $65.00
ASIN: B01M1L6OSX

TUNING THE UKULELE

Tuning the ukulele is a tricky thing to do at first, since each string needs to be tuned to a particular music tone which involves very detailed adjustments by turning the tuning pegs very slowly one way or the other. It is usually a good idea to purchase an automatic tuner which will show if the strings are tuned too high or too low, until they are correctly tuned.

Each string should be tuned to a particular music tone.

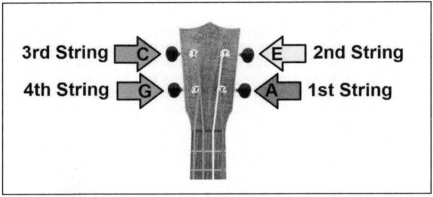

Turn the tuning pegs very slowly one way or the other to tune the strings to a higher or lower tone.

Many tuners like this one will clip on to the ukulele's head and automatically sense the musical tones when the strings are played "open", or without any fingers on it. The tuner will show if the string is tuned too low, too high, or correctly in tune.

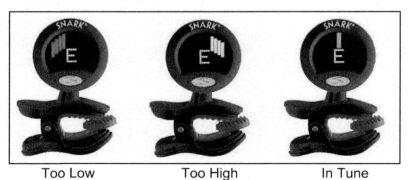

Too Low   Too High   In Tune

UKULELE BASICS
The Fretboard

Most standard ukuleles have four strings.

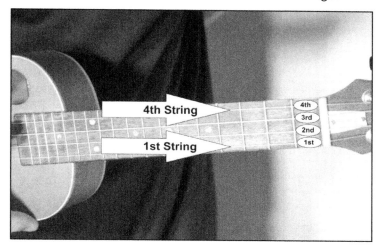

The spaces on the neck of the ukulele are called the **Frets**.

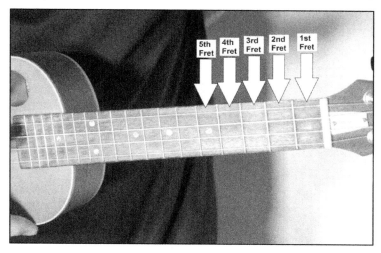

The Strings and Frets on the neck of the ukulele are often called the **Fretboard**.

FINGERS & FRETS

A ukulele player's fingers are numbered accordingly, with the index or pointer finger as the first finger, the middle finger as the second, ring finger as the third, and little or pinky finger as the fourth.

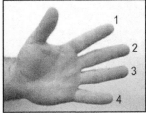

Finger Numbers

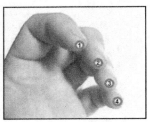

Fingertips

Press and hold your fingertips directly on the strings along the frets, and then pluck or strum the strings with your other hand using your thumb or a guitar pick to make music notes.

FRETBOARD DIAGRAMS

Fretboard Diagrams show a grid which represents the strings and frets on the ukulele:

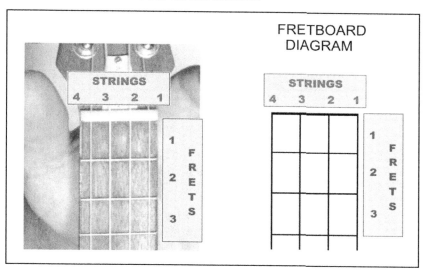

A zero "O" above the grid tells you to play that string "open", or without any fingers on it.

1st String, Open:

3rd String, Open:

The numbered circles on the grid tell you which Finger to press on the indicated String and Fret.

(**TIP**: Use your finger tip precisely to press down hard on the string and fret indicated. Your fingers may be a bit sore at first, but eventually they will get used to it.)

First Finger on 1st String, 1st Fret:

Second Finger on 3rd String, 2nd Fret:

ONE FINGER CHORDS

A **CHORD** in music is the sound of three or more musical notes being played at the same time.

An easy way to get started playing chords on the ukulele is to play simpler one finger chords.

Here's how:

The C7 chord:

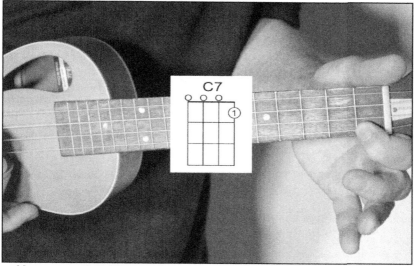

Use your 1st Finger to press on the 1st String, 1st Fret,
and then use your other hand to
play or strum all the strings together at the same time
with your thumb or a pick.

(NOTE: The "O"s on the grid tell you to also strum the 2nd, 3rd and 4th Strings "open" together with your finger on the 1st String.

The C chord:

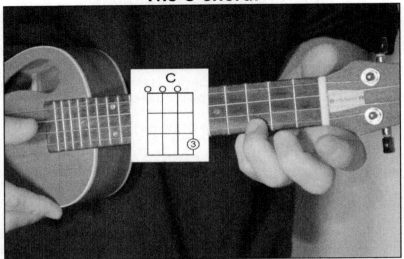

Use your 3rd Finger to press on the 1st String, 3rd Fret,
and then use your other hand to
play or strum all the strings together at the same time
with your thumb or a pick.

Practice strumming the C & C7 chords several times to get a nice clear sound, changing back and forth from one chord to the other.

Next, practice strumming each chord four times slowly and steadily, changing back and forth from C to C7.

Strum Marks

Sometimes slashes, or strum marks, are used to show that the same chord should be strummed again, or repeated.

C   C   C   C   C7   C7   C7   C7

. . . is the same as . . .

C   /   /   /   G7   /   /   /

(**TIP**: Keep a slow and steady regular pattern when strumming chords. This is also called keeping a steady **rhythm**.)

STRUMMING RHYTHMS

Practice these strums with a C or C7 chord:

> Keep A Steady Rhythm
Start counting a slow and steady four counts, about one second each:

1 . . . 2 . . . 3 . . . 4 . . .

Now use your thumb or a pick to strum downward across all the strings on the count of 1, then just hold the chord but don't strum for the counts of 2 . . . 3 . . . 4 . . . (Repeat several times)

> Strum On Each Count
Next, use the same slow and steady 4 count rhythm, but strum down on every count:

1 . . . 2 . . . 3 . . . 4 . . .
strum . . . strum . . . strum . . . strum . . .

> Same Tempo But Twice The Strums
Now, keep the same tempo, or speed, but start strumming down on every half count, using "and" in between to keep it steady:

1 - and - 2 - and - 3 - and - 4 - and -
strum - strum - strum - strum - strum - strum - strum - strum

> Down, *Down-Up*   *(A Great Ukulele Strum!)*
Again, keep the same steady tempo, or speed, but start counting it as:

1 *- and a -* 2 *- and a -* 3 *- and a -* 4 *- and a -*
strumming
down, *down-up*, **down**, *down-up*, **down**, *down-up*, **down**, *down-up*,

(**TIP**: On the *down-up* part, quickly *swipe* up across the strings as your hand comes back up after the down strum every other time.)

THE G7 CHORD

Three finger chords take a little more work, but if you can learn this next one, you'll be able to start playing some songs right away.

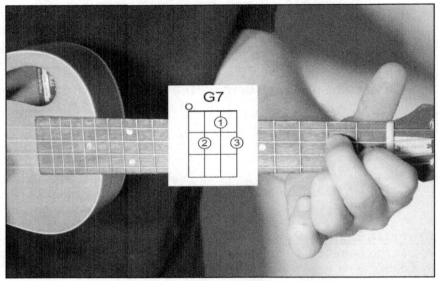

Put your 1st Finger on 2nd String, 1st Fret,
. . . then also put your 2nd Finger on 3rd String, 2nd Fret,
. . . and also put your 3rd Finger on 1st String, 2nd Fret.

NOTE: The "O" means that the 4th String is also strummed "open".

When you have all three fingers in place, press down and strum all the strings together.

Practice this chord several times, taking your fingers off and then putting them back on and strumming again, until you start to have it memorized.

Now you're ready to play a few songs!

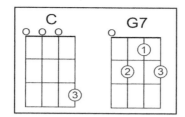

MARY HAD A LITTLE LAMB

C / / / G7 / C /
Mary had a lit-tle lamb, lit-tle lamb, lit-tle lamb,

C / / / G7 / C
Mary had a lit-tle lamb, its fleece was white as snow.

ARE YOU SLEEPING?

C / / / C / / /
Are you sleeping, are you sleeping? Brother John, Brother John?

C / C /
Morning bells are ringing, morning bells are ringing,

C - G7 - C C - G7 - C
Ding ding dong, ding ding dong.

LONDON BRIDGE

C / / / G7 / C /
London Bridge is falling down, falling down, falling down,

C / / / G7 / C
London Bridge is falling down, my fair lady.

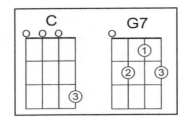

THE MULBERRY BUSH

C   /   /   /
Here we go round   the   mulberry   bush

G7   /   /   /
The mulberry bush,   the mulberry   bush

C   /   /   /
Here we go round   the   mulberry   bush   so

G7   /   C   /
Ear - ly   in   the   mor - ning.

***

ROW, ROW, ROW YOUR BOAT

C   /   /   /
Row, row, row your boat

C   /   /   /
Gently down the stream,

C   /   /   /
Merrily merrily, merrily, merrily

G7   /   C
Life is but a dream

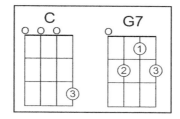

SKIP TO MY LOU

C   /   /   /
Choose your partner, skip to my lou

G7   /   /   /
Choose your partner, skip to my lou

C   /   /   /
Choose your partner, skip to my lou

G7   /   C   /
Skip to my lou, my dar - ling.

C   /   /   /
Can't get a red bird, blue bird'll do,

G7   /   /   /
Can't get a red bird, blue bird'll do,

C   /   /   /
Can't get a red bird, blue bird'll do,

G7   /   C   /
Skip to my lou, my dar - ling.

THE MOCKINGBIRD SONG

```
C              /          G7          /
Hush,    little ba - by,      don't   say a word,
G7             /          C           /
Mama's going to buy you a mock-ing-bird.
C              /          G7          /
And if that mockingbird won't sing,
G7             /          C           /
Mama's going to buy you a diamond ring.
C              /          G7          /
And if that diamond ring turns brass,
G7             /          C           /
Mama's going to buy you a looking glass.
C              /          G7          /
And if that looking glass gets broke,
G7             /          C           /
Mama's going to buy you a billy    goat.
C              /          G7          /
And if that billy    goat won't pull,
G7             /          C           /
Mama's going to buy you a cart and bull.
C              /          G7          /
And if that cart and bull turns over,
G7             /          C           /
Mama's going to buy you a dog named Rover.
C              /          G7          /
And if that dog named Rover won't bark,
G7             /          C           /
Mama's going to buy you a horse and cart.
C              /          G7          /
And if that horse and cart falls down,
G7             /          C           /
You'll still be the sweetest little baby in town.
```

***

THE F CHORD

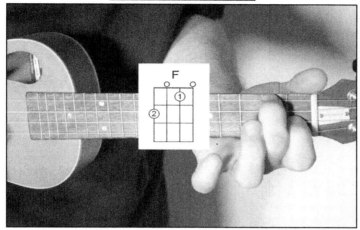

Put your 1st Finger on 2nd String, 1st Fret,
. . . then also put your 2nd Finger on 4th String, 2nd Fret,
. . . the 1st and 3rd Strings are also strummed open (O).

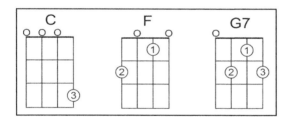

THIS OLD MAN

```
C              /           /              /
This   old   man,        he   played   one,
F              /         G7              /
he played   knick knack    on   my   thumb, with a
C              /           /              /
knick knack, paddy whack, give the dog a bone,
G7             /           /              C
This   old   man   came   rolling   home.
```

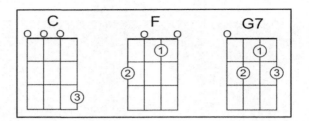

<u>SILENT NIGHT</u>

```
C              C           C           C
Si  - lent    night . . .  ho - ly    night,

G              G           C           C
all       is  calm . . .   all     is  bright

F              F           C           C
Round   yon vir  - gin,    mo - ther and child

F              F           C           C
Ho  - ly      in - fant so ten - der and mild;

G              G           C           C
Sleep     in hea – ven-ly pea   -   ce,

C              G           C
Sle - ep in    hea - ven-ly peace.
```

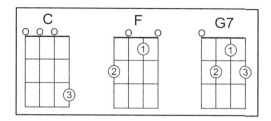

WHEN THE SAINTS GO MARCHING IN

C   /   /   /
Oh, when the saints . . .   go marching

C   /   /   /
in . . .   Oh when the

C   /   /   /
saints go march-ing

G7   /   /   /
in . . .   Lord, I

C   /   /   /
want   to be   in that

F   /   /   /
number . . .   When the

C   /   G7   /
saints go march-ing

C   /   /
in.

THE G CHORD

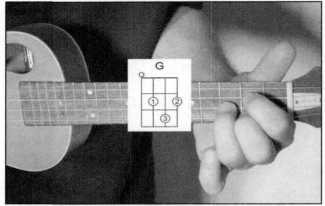

Put your 1st Finger on 3rd String, 2nd Fret,
. . . then also put your 2nd Finger on 1st String, 2nd Fret,
. . . and also put your 3rd Finger on 2nd String, 3rd Fret,
. . . the 4th String is also strummed open (O).

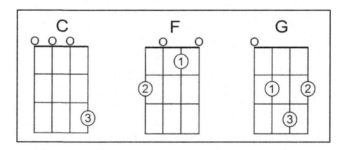

TWINKLE, TWINKLE, LITTLE STAR

C   G   F   C   F   C   G   C
Twinkle, twinkle, little star,   how I wonder what you are.

G   F   C   G   G   F   C   G
Up above the world so high,   like a dia-mond in the sky,

C   G   F   C   F   C   G   C
Twinkle, twinkle, little star,   how I wonder what you are.

THE D CHORD

There are two different ways to play the D chord, so you can decide which way is easiest or better for you. Either way will sound good.

The first way uses three fingers to play three different strings.

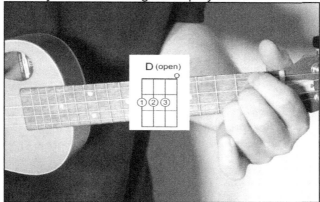

Put your 1st Finger on 4th String, 2nd Fret,
. . . then also put your 2nd Finger on 3rd String, 2nd Fret,
. . . and also put your 3rd Finger on 2nd String, 2nd Fret,
. . . the 4th String is also strummed open (O).

The other way is to use one finger to "**bar**" across the 4th, 3rd and 2nd Strings on the 2nd Fret, but try not to strum the 1st String (X).

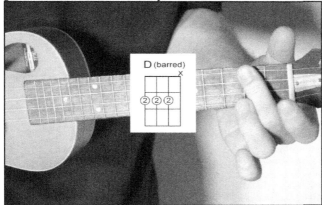

(**TIP**: You can lift up your knuckle slighly on your barred finger to muffle or mute the 1st String as you strum.)

ADVANCED STRUMMING

When it comes to strumming more advanced rhythms on the ukulele, two strum patterns stand out because they are so popular and widely used.

> The first is the **Down, Down-Up, Up-Down-Up** strum.

To get started, do the first part of the strum several times:
Down, Down-Up . . . Down, Down-Up . . . Down, Down-Up . . .

Next, do the second part several times:
Up-Down-Up . . . Up-Down-Up . . . Up-Down-Up . . .

When you're able to do both parts smoothly and steadily,
try strumming both parts together:
Down, Down-Up . . . Up-Down-Up . . .

(**TIP**: Try to keep your arm moving steadily down and up as you strum, especially between the two parts of the strum where your arm should go down without strumming between the two "Ups" to strum up again.)

> The other useful strum is the **Down, Down, Down-Up-Down-Up**.

Once again, the trick is to keep your arm moving steadily down and up to make a smooth rhythm.

Start by strumming steady down strums with a count of
"1 . . . 2 . . . 3 . . . 4 . . ."
Down . . . Down . . . Down . . . Down . . .

Next, keep the same rhythm speed (tempo) but turn your count into
"1 . . . 2 . . . 3 *and* 4 *and* . . .
which becomes:
Down . . . Down . . . Down-*Up*-Down-*Up* . . .

(**TIP**: These advanced strums take a little getting used to, but they are used in lots of songs, so keep practicing them until you can "feel" the rhythm without thinking about the Downs or Ups any more and they become "automatic".)

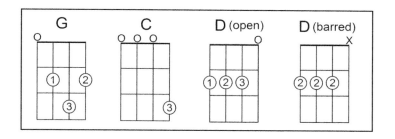

<u>YANKEE DOODLE</u>

```
G            /              /           D
Yan - kee  Do - odle   went   to    town,
G            /              D           /
Rid  -  ing    on    a     po  -  ny
G            /              C           /
Stuck   a   fea - ther   in   his   cap   and
D            /              G           /
called   it   ma  -  ca  -  ro  -  ni.
```

***

<u>AMAZING GRACE</u>

```
   G              /            C           G
A-ma -   zi-ng Grace,   how sweet,   the sound,
   G              /            D           D
that saved,   a wretch,   like me . . . . . . . . . .
   G              /            C           G
I   on- ce,   w-as lost,   but now,   I'-m found,
   G              D            G
was blind,   but now,      I see.
```

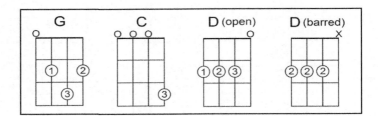

OLD MACDONALD

G   G   C   G
Old Mac - Donald   had   a   farm,

G   D   G   G
E - I - E - I - O.

G   G   C   G
And on this farm   he   had   a   dog,

G   D   G   G
E - I - E - I - O.

        G   (HOLD)
With a   bark, bark   here,

        G   (HOLD)
and a   bark, bark   there,

G   G
Here a bark, there a bark,

G   G
everywhere a bark, bark,

G   G   C   G
Old Mac - Donald   had   a   farm,

G   D   G
E - I - E - I - O.

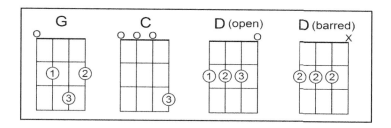

COMING 'ROUND THE MOUNTAIN

G / / /
She'll be coming 'round the mountain when she

G / / /
comes . . . . She'll be

G / / /
coming 'round the mountain when she

D / / /
comes . . . . She'll be

G / / /
coming 'round the mountain, she'll be

C / / /
coming 'round the mountain, she'll be

D / / /
coming 'round the mountain when she

G / /
comes.

THE A CHORD

Put your 1st Finger on 3rd String, 1st Fret,
. . . then also put your 2nd Finger on the 4th String, 2nd Fret,
. . . the 1st & 2nd Strings are also strummed open (O).

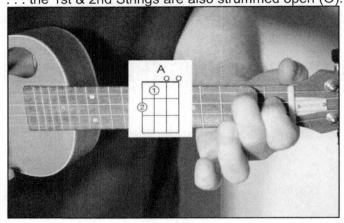

D (open)	D (barred)	G	A

DO YOU KNOW THE MUFFIN MAN?

D   /   /   /
Oh, do you know the muffin man,

G   /   A   /
the muffin man, the muffin man

D   /   /   /
Oh do you know the muffin man,

G   A   D
Who lives on Drury Lane?

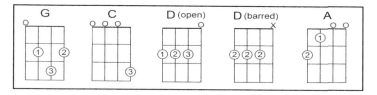

JINGLE BELLS

```
G              /              /              /
Dashing   through the snow . . . . . . . in a
G              /              C              /
one    horse open    sleigh . . . . . . . . . . .
C              /              D              /
O'er the    fields    we    go . . . . . . . . . . . .
D              /              G              /
laughing    all    the    way . . . . . . . . . . . . .
G              /              /              /
Bells    on    bobtail    ring . . . . . . . . . . . . .
G              /              C              /
making    spirits    bright . . . . . . . . . . . What
C              /              D              /
fun      it    is    to    ride    and    sing    a
D              /              G              D
Sleighing    song    to - night . . . . . . . Oh,
G              /              /              /
Jin - gle    bells . . . . . . . Jin - gle    bells,
G              /              /              /
Jin - gle    all    the    way . . . . . . . . . .
C              /              G              /
Oh,    what fun         it    is    to    ride    in a
A              /              D              /
one    horse op - en    sleigh . . . . . . . Hey!
G              /              /              /
Jin - gle    bells . . . . . . . Jin - gle    bells,
G              /              /              /
Jin - gle    all    the    way . . . . . . . . . .
C              /              G              /
Oh,    what fun         it    is    to    ride    in a
D              /              G
one horse op - en    sleigh.
```

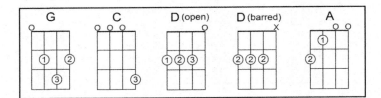

I'VE BEEN WORKING ON THE RAILROAD

G   /   /   /
I've been working on the rail-road

C   /   G   /
All the live long day . . . .

G   /   /   /
I've been working on the rail-road

A   /   D   /
Just to pass the time away . . . .

D   /   G   /
Can't you hear the whistle blowing

C   /   G   /
Rise up so early in the morn . . . . . .

C   /   G   /
Can't you hear the whistle blowing

D   /   G   /
Dinah, blow your horn . . . .

G   /   C   /
Dinah won't you blow, Dinah won't you blow

D   /   G   /
Dinah, won't you blow your horn . . . .

G   /   C   /
Dinah won't you blow, Dinah won't you blow

D   /   G   /
Dinah, won't you blow your horn.

A7 & D7 CHORDS

The A7 Chord
Put your 1st Finger on 3rd String, 1st Fret,
. . . the 1st, 2nd & 4th Strings are also strummed open (O).

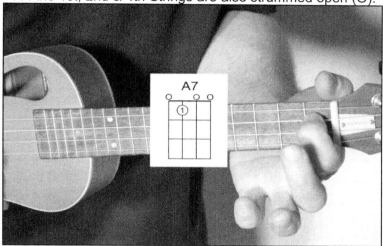

The D7 Chord
Bar your 1st Finger across the 4th, 3rd & 2nd Strings on the 2nd Fret,
. . . then also put your 3rd (or 2nd) Finger on 1st String, 3rd Fret.

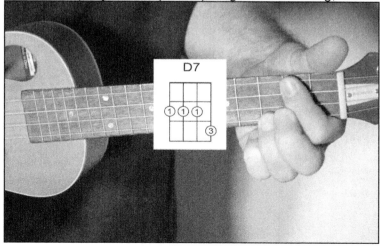

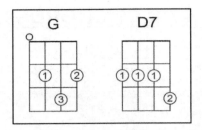

OH, MY DARLING, CLEMENTINE

```
    G       /       /       G       /       /
In a ca - vern,    In   a   can - yon,   ex-ca

    G       /       /       D7      /       /
va  -   ting  for   a   mine,        Dwelt a

    D7      /       /       G       /       /
mi  -  ner  forty  -  ni - ner,      and  his

    D7      /       /       G       /       /
daugh - ter  Clemen - tine . . . . . . .  Oh my

    G       /       /       G       /       /
dar - ling,   Oh  my  dar - ling,    Oh my

    G       /       /       D7      /       /
dar  -  ling  Clemen - tine,          You are

    D7      /       /       G       /       /
lost   and   gone  for - e - ver,  dreadf-ul

    D7      /       /       G
sor-   ry   Clemen - tine.
```

***

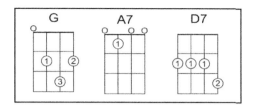

OH! SUSANNA

G   /   /   /
I come from Alabama with my

A7   /   D7   /
banjo   on   my   knee .   .   .

G   /   /   /
I'm   going   to   Louisiana, my

D7   /   G   /
true   love   for   to   see.

G   /   /   /
It rained all night the day I left, the

A7   /   D7   /
weather   it   was   dry .   .   .

G   /   /   /
The sun so hot I froze to death,

D7   /   G   /
Susanna, don't you cry.

C   /   /   /
Oh!   Su - sanna,   Oh

G   A7   D7   /
don't you cry for me, for I

G   /   /   /
come from Alabama with my

D7   /   G
banjo on my knee.

Dm, E & Em CHORDS

The Dm Chord

1st Finger on 2nd String, 1st Fret,

2nd Finger on 4th String, 2nd Fret,

3rd Finger on 3rd String, 2nd Fret,

The 1st String is also strummed open (O).

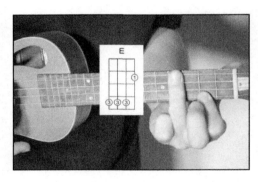

The E Chord

1st Finger on 1st String, 2nd Fret,

Use 3rd Finger to bar across 4th, 3rd & 2nd Strings on 4th Fret.

(*You might have to lift your barred knuckle slightly to avoid barring the 1st String.*)

The Em Chord

1st Finger on 1st String, 2nd Fret,

2nd Finger on 2nd String, 3rd Fret,

3rd Finger on 3rd String, 4th Fret,

The 4th String is also strummed open (O).

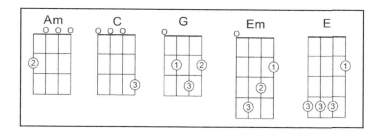

<u>GREENSLEEVES</u>
(What Child Is This?)

    Am   C   G   Em
What Child   is   this   who laid   to rest,

    Am   Am   E   E
on   Ma - ry's lap   is sleep - ing?

    Am   C   G   Em
Whom an - gels greet   with an - thems sweet,

    Am   E   Am   Am
while shep-herds watch   are   keep - ing?

    C   C   G   G
  This,   this   is   Christ the King,

    Am   Am   E   E
whom shep-herds guard and an - gels sing

    C   C   G   G
  Haste,   haste,   to bring Him laud,

    Am   E   Am   Am
the babe, the son   of Ma - ry.

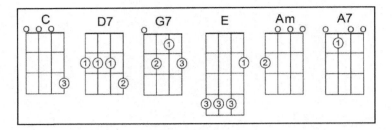

AURA LEE

```
C           /           D7          /
As the black - bird    in the spring

G7          /           C           /
'neath the wil-low    tree . . . . .

C           /           D7          /
sat and piped    I heard him sing

G7          /           C           /
praising  Aura   Lee . . . . . . . .

C           /           E           /
Aura    Lee!      Aura      Lee!

Am          /           E           /
Maid   of   golden   hair . . . . .

C           A7          D7          /
sunshine came along with thee

G7          /           C
and swall-ows in the air.
```

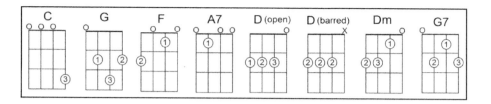

AMERICA THE BEAUTIFUL

C   /   G   /   F   G   C   /
O beau - ti-ful   for spac- -ious skies, for am-ber waves of grain,

C   /   G   /   A7   /   D   /
For pur-ple moun-tain maj-es-ties,   A-bove the fruit-ed plain.

C   /   G   /   Dm   G   C   /
A-mer- -i-ca!   A-mer- -i-ca!   God shed his grace on thee

F   /   C   /   F   G7   C
And crown, thy good with bro- therhood, from sea to shin-ing sea!

***

CHORD INDEX

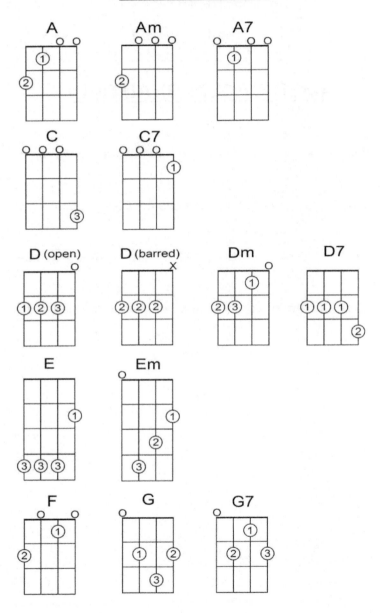

Printed in Great Britain
by Amazon

49825795R00030